Library of
Davidson College

The American Revolutionary Series

THE LOYALIST LIBRARY

*The American Revolutionary Series
is published in cooperation with
The Boston Public Library*

The Legacy of the American Revolution to the British West Indies and Bahamas: A Chapter out of the History of the American Loyalists

By
WILBUR H. SIEBERT

With a New Introduction and Preface by
GEORGE ATHAN BILLIAS

GREGG PRESS
Boston 1972

This is a complete photographic reprint of a work first published in Columbus, Ohio, by the Ohio State University in 1913. Reproduced from an original copy in the Boston Public Library.

First Gregg Press edition published 1972.

Printed on permanent/durable acid-free paper in The United States of America.

973.31
S571l

Library of Congress Cataloging in Publication Data

Siebert, Wilbur Henry, 1866-1961.
   The legacy of the American revolution to the British West Indies and Bahamas.
   (American Revolutionary series)
   Reprint of the 1913 ed.
   1. West Indies, British—History. 2. Bahamas—History. 3. American loyalists. I. Title. II. Series.
F2131.S56   1972   973.3'14   72-8754
ISBN 0-8398-1886-6

THE LOYALIST LIBRARY

THE LOYALISTS in the American Revolution represent one of the most misunderstood groups in our nation's history. For the past two centuries, they have fared badly at the hands of historians; Tories have either been neglected, or protrayed in an unsympathetic light by ultra-patriotic writers. The remark that a Loyalist was "a thing whose head is in England... body... in America, and its neck ought to be stretched," typifies the common attitude during the first century after the Revolution. This early period was one of outspoken nationalism, and resentment against the Loyalists and former mother country remained high. Although Anglo-American animosities diminished in the second century, and scholars adopted a more detached approach, the Tories were studied only sporadically. The present collection—called the Loyalist Library—contains both writings of important Tories and scholarly monographs on the subject. It should help to stimulate renewed research and interest in this forgotten part of America's past.

History is usually written by winners, not losers, and therefore we do not know as much about the Loyalists as we should. For one thing, we do not know how many Tories there actually were. The old estimate—mistakenly attributed to John Adams—claimed that the country was split three ways during the war: one-third becoming

Loyalists; one-third supporting the patriot cause; and one-third remaining neutral or indifferent. Modern scholars estimate that the Tories comprised something closer to nineteen percent of the total number of white Americans. Several studies included in this collection, such as Otis G. Hammond's *Tories of New Hampshire,* and Janet B. Johnson's biography of Robert Alexander, a Maryland Loyalist, provide evidence that casts serious doubts on the older assumption.

The Loyalist Library should help to correct another misconception—the idea that Tories came mainly from the upper class—from the ranks of royal officeholders, rich merchants, professional men, and well-to-do Anglicans. Recent research into the socio-economic background of Tories reveals that they hailed instead from the middle or lower classes in most of the colonies. Farmers, artisans, and small businessmen formed the backbone of the Loyalist movement for the most part. Wilbur H. Siebert's work on *The Loyalists of Pennsylvania,* for example, shows that in the Quaker colony many frontier farmers became Tories.

In geographical terms, the Loyalists were scattered throughout all of the original thirteen colonies. Virginia and Massachusetts had the smallest number. The strongest Tory support seems to have been in certain of the Middle Colonies—New York, New Jersey, and Pennsylvania—and in the South—in the Carolinas and Georgia. State studies of these areas, such as Edward Alfred Jones' *The Loyalists of New Jersey* and Harold B. Hancock's *The Delaware Loyalists,* tell us specifically who the Tories were—their names, place of residence, occupation or profession, and religion. Loyalists, moreover, tended to concentrate in urban areas and along the seacoast—except in New York, North Carolina, and parts of Pennsylvania where major pockets of Tories could be found in the interior. The treatment that Tories received at the hands of the Whigs in such seacoast cities as Boston may be gleaned from Arthur W. Eaton's biography of Mather Byles.

The Loyalist Library also provides proof that the Floridas and Nova Scotia—none of which rebelled—may have held the highest ratio of Tories. Wilbur H. Siebert's *Loyalists in East Florida, 1774 to 1785* indicates that the number of Tories in that colony increased substantially as a result of the exodus from the Carolinas and Georgia. The papers of Edward Winslow reflect the problems that incoming Loyalists encountered in resettling in Nova Scotia.

It is estimated that seventy-five to eighty thousand Loyalists left the United States during the war for England, Canada, the West Indies, and other parts of the British empire. Pamphlets of refugees like Joseph Galloway, which are reprinted here, reveal much about the views of the Loyalists who went to England. Some individuals remained men without a country, and lived out their days in London while dreaming about America. Others took up careers on the continent, as is evident in George E. Ellis' *Memoir of Sir Benjamin Thompson, Count Rumford*. Another major group—the United Empire Loyalists—whose story is presented in certain of these writings, settled in Canada and became the founding fathers of new communities.

The Loyalist Library includes also valuable primary source materials. Loyalist letters, pamphlets, and personal narratives help to shed light on the key question: Why did the American Tories remain loyal to their King? Prominent Loyalists like Daniel Leonard of Massachusetts and Joseph Galloway of Pennsylvania explain their political position in their writings. They tell us what they considered to be the proper relationship between colonies and mother country, the King and his subjects, and colonial governors and the American people. Until we view the Loyalists as men with "positive political ideas" and individuals capable of "creative statesmanship," a balanced interpretation of the Revolution will elude us, says one historian.

The Loyalist Library, then, is a combination of primary source documents and secondary materials. It includes private letters, diaries, and narratives, Tory histories and pamphlets, as well as scholarly books written on the subject. The collection makes available certain sources that were heretofore less accessible, and it should enable students to become more familiar with the Loyalist side of the story of the Revolution.

PREFACE

ONE OF THE most poignant eipsodes in the Revolution was the Tory exodus from America. Loyalists began seeking safety in flight as early as 1774. They scattered in all directions, some finding their way to the Bahamas and other British possessions in the West Indies. Wilbur H. Siebert, one of the most devoted scholars of the Loyalists, has produced in this significant work a study tracing the migration to the Caribbean.

These Loyalist exiles, Siebert descovered, did not always go directly from America to the West Indies islands. They often sought asylum first in East or West Florida. From the outset of the war, East Florida served as a retreat for Loyalist refugees from the Carolinas and Georgia. The number of Tories in East Florida jumped sharply when the British evacuated Savannah in July, 1782. A second influx into the area occurred when more than 3,800 persons came from Charleston when the British left that post in December of 1782. Siebert estimates that at least 7,300 persons, many of them slaves of wealthy planters, were involved in these two migrations.

West Florida, which was a greater distance from neighboring Southern Colonies, received its Loyalist exiles from further north. Some were Tories serving with the British military forces and hailed from Maryland and Pennsylvania. When West Florida was subjugated by the Spanish during the war, many Loyalists fled to the Bahamas, other British West Indies possessions, and to other parts of the empire.

Not all the Loyalists in the West Indies came by way of the Floridas, however. When Savannah was evacuated, many refugees eventually made their way to Jamaica. The abandonment of Charleston caused almost 3,900 persons to embark directly for Jamaica. There were also cases of Massachusetts Tories settling in Antigua and St. Christophers. In the post-war period, moreover, numbers of Loyalist exiled to Nova Scotia left to resettle in Jamaica and other islands.

The Bahamas, which were won and then lost by Spain during the war, provided an asylum for large numbers of Loyalists. Many Tories migrated from East Florida to the Bahamas in the years 1783-1785. Siebert estimates that between 6,000 and 7,000 whites and blacks entered the Bahamas during that period.

Jamaica likewise attracted numerous Loyalists, many settling in the community of Kingston. In the main these Tories came from the Southern Colonies, but a few migrated from Massachusetts, Connecticut, New York, and Pennsylvania. Little is known about the Loyalists in Jamaica, though many of them appear to have been slaveholders. When the Jamaica Assembly passed legislation to help the refugees settle in their new homes, there was considerable resentment on the part of certain older inhabitants.

Siebert's study of the dispersion of Loyalists to the British West Indies represents a pioneering effort which, in many instances, has not yet been improved upon.

George Athan Billias
Clark University

Volume XVII   Number 27

The Ohio State University Bulletin

The Legacy of the American Revolution to the British West Indies and Bahamas

A Chapter out of the History of the American Loyalists

April, 1913

PUBLISHED BY THE UNIVERSITY AT COLUMBUS

Entered as second-class matter November 17, 1905, at the postoffice at Columbus, Ohio, under Act of Congress, July 16, 1894

THE OHIO STATE UNIVERSITY

The Ohio State University, located at Columbus, is a part of the public educational facilities maintained by the State. It comprises seven colleges and a graduate school:

>The College of Agriculture,
>The College of Arts, Philosophy, and Science,
>The College of Education,
>The College of Engineering,
>The College of Law,
>The College of Pharmacy,
>The College of Veterinary Medicine,
>The Graduate School.

[NOTE: The University publishes a bulletin descriptive of each college. Copies may be obtained by addressing W. E. Mann, University Editor, Columbus, Ohio, and stating the college in which the writer is interested.]

The Ohio State University Bulletin is published at least twenty times during the year as follows: Monthly in July, August, September and June, and bi-weekly in October, November, December, January, February, March, April and May.

The Legacy of the American Revolution to the British West Indies and Bahamas

A Chapter out of the History of the American Loyalists

BY

WILBUR H. SIEBERT, A. M.
Professor of European History

Published by
The Ohio State University
Columbus
1913

Copyrighted, 1913, by
WILBUR H. SIEBERT

Contents

I. THE LOYALISTS IN EAST FLORIDA

	PAGE
The organization of loyalist regiments in and for East Florida	6
Number of refugees in East Florida increased by the evacuation of Savannah	7
Further increase of East Florida's population on the evacuation of Charleston	8
St. Augustine experiences a visitation of loyal Indians	9
Attitude of the British government towards the Indians	10
Unwillingness of loyalist regiments to remove from East Florida	11

II. THE LOYALISTS IN WEST FLORIDA

West Florida as a refuge for loyalists	11
Loyalist defenders of West Florida	12
What became of the loyalists of West Florida	13

III. THE EMIGRATION OF LOYALISTS TO JAMAICA

Early movement of refugees to the West Indies and Bahamas	14
Emigration from Savannah to Jamaica and other places	14
Emigration from Charleston to Jamaica	15
Incompleteness of our information concerning the loyalist emigration from East Florida to Jamaica	15
Exodus from Honduras, the Mosquito Shore, and other places to Jamaica	16

IV. THE LOYALISTS IN THE BAHAMAS

Spain gains and loses the Bahamas	16
Efforts to retain East Florida as an asylum for the loyalists	17

	PAGE
Visit to New Providence by intending settlers and by Lieutenant Wilson	18
Report by Lieutenant Wilson on the availability of the Bahamas for colonization	19
Movement of loyalists from East Florida to the Bahamas, 1783-1785	19
Colonization of Great Abaco Island by loyalists	20
Increase in population of the Bahamas by immigration of the loyalists	22
Adventures of Colonel David Fanning	22
Conditions in the Island of Great Abaco	24
Effects of the loyalist immigration on political conditions in the Bahamas	25
Effects of the movement on the commercial conditions in the islands	26
Effects on agriculture in the islands	27
How plantation life in the Bahamas was affected by the loyalists	29
Attitude of Parliament towards slavery in the Bahama Islands	31
The Wylly affair	31
The struggle over an improved slave code for the Bahamas	33
The end of slavery in the islands	33

V. THE LOYALISTS IN JAMAICA

Sir John Temple's plan to colonize the loyalists in Porto Rico	34
Legislation in Jamaica for the benefit of the loyalists	35
Protest against the new legislation by older inhabitants of Jamaica	36
Distribution of loyalists in Jamaica	37
States from which they came, and classes represented among them	38
Experiences of Dr. William Martin Johnson and his family before and after settling in Jamaica	39
Life of the loyalists in Jamaica and the other British West Indies	41
Slavery in Jamaica	43

VI. THE LOSSES AND COMPENSATION OF THE LOYALISTS IN THE ISLANDS

PAGE

Losses of loyalist settlers in the islands illustrated by those of many refugees in Jamaica......................... 44
Parliament's measures for the relief of the claimants from East Florida... 45
Compensation of individual refugees in the islands........ 46
Appointment of loyalists to office in the islands............ 47

The Legacy of the American Revolution to the British West Indies and Bahamas

A Chapter out of the History of the American Loyalists

I. The Loyalists in East Florida

From the beginning of the Revolutionary War, East Florida served as a retreat for loyalist refugees from the Carolinas and Georgia. As early as 1776, Lieutenant-Colonel Thomas Brown, himself a fugitive from Savannah, formed a regiment, in whole or in part, of these refugees, which he called the East Florida Rangers. This he supplemented in the spring of 1778, by engaging three hundred and fifty men from the same colonies to defend the frontiers of the peninsula. These men were organized at first into a regiment known as the South Carolina Royalists under the command of Colonel Innes, and the next year were re-organized as a regiment of infantry under the title of the King's Rangers.[1] They formed part of the English force in East Florida, as recounted by a deserter on his arrival at Charleston in the early summer of the same year, a force which, he said, also included eight hundred regular troops, one hundred Florida Rangers, one hundred and fifty provincial militia, and two hundred Indians.[2] All told Colonel Brown enlisted as many as twelve hundred men, if we may credit his own statement in a letter to Sir Guy Carleton, and of these he proudly asserted that five hundred were killed in the course of the constant and distant service in which he and his men were engaged throughout the War.[3] Doubtless most of his recruits were gathered in Georgia and the Carolinas, where he conducted his campaigns.

1. *Report on the Am. Mss. in the Roy. Inst. of G. Brit.*, *III*, 322, 323; McCall, *History of Georgia*, 72.
2. McCall, *History of Georgia*, 421.
3. *Report on the Am. Mss. in the Roy. Inst. of G. Brit.*, *III*, 323.

The loyalist element in East Florida was greatly increased by the evacuations of Savannah and Charleston. The former event occurred in July, 1782, 7,000 persons being turned adrift between the twelfth and twenty-fifth of that month. This host was made up of twelve hundred British regulars and loyalists, five hundred women and children, three hundred Indians, and five thousand negroes. Three months later, Patrick Tonyn, governor of East Florida, wrote Carleton that the number of settlers in his province previous to the surrender of Georgia was "about a thousand and near three thousand blacks," that the militia numbered about three hundred, and that some five hundred of the negroes might be entrusted with arms. "The Refugees from Georgia," he said, "are about fifteen hundred whites and a thousand negroes; there are a few respectable families but they consist chiefly of backwoodsmen who are intolerably indolent; perhaps about four hundred may be found fit to bear arms, but their appearance is against them, their families are in distress, and they are exceedingly dissatisfied. The provincial corps no doubt may be completed from them."[1]

Prompt measures were taken to alleviate the condition of these people and to ascertain fully their number. Already, Colonel Brown was engaged in pointing out lands to them and establishing them in settlements on the St. John's River, and Brigadier-General Archibald McArthur, who was in command in East Florida, soon designated a committee of four of the principal refugees—Colonels Ball and Cassells for the Carolinas and Colonels Tattnall and Douglas for Georgia to take a census of them and to superintend the distribution of provisions among them. By the end of October, their numbers were not yet fully ascertained, for not all had been able to land on account of the bad weather and the dangerous bar in the harbor of St. Augustine.[2] Meanwhile, an inspector of refugees seemed a necessity, and John Winniett was appointed to that office. His first report covered arrivals from July to the thirteenth of November, 1782, exclusive of those

1. *Report on the Am. Mss. in the Roy. Inst. of G. Brit.*, III, 163, 164
2. Ibid., 140, 192.

who had come in before that period, and showed a total of 3,340 refugees and slaves.[1]

Although the evacuation of Charleston did not occur until December 24, numbers of loyalists, military and civilian, were already being sent from that place to St. Augustine by the middle of the previous month. Among these were the North and South Carolina regiments, the King's Rangers, and a body of refugees described as "distinguished loyalists" by Governor Tonyn, many of whom, he said, were substantial merchants and planters. He accommodated the merchants with houses in town and placed the planters on lands, which, although previously granted by the Crown, had not been cultivated, as required by the terms of the grant;[2] and as provisions were being supplied by the government, the chief need of the new settlers was plantation tools. This was the cause of considerable anxiety on the part of the provincial authorities, and so also was the tendency of the refugees to concentrate in St. Augustine and at a place on the St. John's River known as the Bluff. Both Governor Tonyn and General McArthur exerted themselves to prevent this concentration.[3] By the middle of December, Charleston passed into the possession of the Americans and witnessed the unhappy departure of 9,121 persons, not counting the troops. Of this number 3,826 embarked for East Florida, 1,615 being whites and 2,211 blacks. On December 23, Inspector Winniett submitted a second enumeration of the refugees and their slaves from Georgia and the Carolinas: according to its figures, the whites now numbered 2,428 and the negroes 3,609, making a total of 6,037.[5] By this time, the loyalists who had come with the first convoy were forming their settlements in the country, and the much needed tools were being supplied them. One division of the fleet of transports, under escort of the *Bellisarius*, was reported to have brought in a thousand loyalists and fifteen hundred negroes. In

    1. *Report on the Am. Mss. in the Roy. Inst. of G. Brit.*, *III*. 216.
    2. *Ibid.*, 64, 112, 220.
    3. *Ibid.*, *III*, 224.
    4. *South Carolina Historical and Genealogical Magazine, Jan., 1910*; *Mass. Historical Society Miscellaneous Papers, 1769-1793*, *V*, 139; McCrady *History of South Carolina*, 674.
    5. *Report on the Am. Mss. in the Roy. Inst. of G. Brit.*, *III*, 276.

disembarking, some small craft were lost "owing to their rashness in venturing over the bar without sufficient guides."[1] A similar fate awaited nine of the vessels in the train of the *Bellisarius*, when she arrived off the bar on her return trip on December 31. Of the 1,300 passengers aboard this fleet, but four were lost.[2] Inspector Winniet completed a third enumeration before these 1,300 landed; but as its figures are unknown, we are only sure of the minimum number of arrivals in East Florida during the period from July, 1782, to the end of the same year, namely, over 7,300.[3] That this number is far short of the actual gain in the population of the province through the incoming of the loyalists is indicated by the contrasted statements of Governor Tonyn and General McArthur. In October, 1782, as we have already seen, the former gave the population as about 1,000 whites and 2,000 blacks before the emigration from Georgia. Seven months later, that is, in May, 1783, his military colleague stated that the population was about 16,000, the proportion between the two races being nearly three blacks to two whites. By this time, it was known of course that the province was to be surrendered to Spain. If, on the other hand, it had been retained, and the large land grants to absentees could be abolished, McArthur thought that East Florida would soon flourish through the presence of the great number of people lately arrived. He reported that since the evacuation of Charleston, a little town, regularly laid out, was forming at the Bluff on St. John's River, which would have soon risen to consequence on account of the harbor being safer there than at St. Augustine. As St. Mary's River possessed the same advantage, he was convinced that numbers of people would have formed a town there also.[4] However, these were prophesies that were not to be fulfilled under loyalist auspices.

In the midst of their labors for the disembarking multitudes, the provincial officers were destined to experience a visitation of Indians from far and near. The question of provisions was already a pressing one when this visitation took place in the latter part of December, 1782. Not only hundreds of Cherokees, Creeks, and Choctaws came to St. Augustine, but also a great deputation from Detroit, on behalf of the Northern Indian nations.

1. *Report on the Am. Mss. in the Roy. Inst. of G. Brit.*, *III*, 276.
2. *Ibid.*, 319, 395.
3. *Ibid.*, 294, 320.
4. *Ibid.*, *IV*, 97, 98.

According to Tonyn, this deputation comprised representatives of the Mohawks, Senecas, Delawares, Shawnees, Mingoes, Tuscarawas, and other tribes. The Cherokee delegation numbered twelve hundred and that of the Choctaws and Chicesaws, six hundred.[1] We can only surmise what may have been the size of the Northern deputation. Fortunately, they came on a peaceful mission, professing themselves firmly attached to the king's interest and commissioned to confirm the southern tribes in the same sentiments.[2] Conferences followed between these people and the Indian department, in which the Indians made it clear that they considered their engagements with England as having been fulfilled, and hoped that they would not be abandoned by the great King. Lieutenant-Colonel Brown, who was superintendent of Indian affairs, gave assurances of Britain's continued attachment to her allies, and recommended them to desist from further offensive operations and to devote themselves to hunting and trading. He also obtained promises from the Cherokees that they would remove their towns at once to a greater distance from the frontiers of Pennsylvania, Virginia, and the Carolinas, so as to be less exposed to attack. Meantime, he managed to keep all of his visitors well supplied with provisions, and he did not forget to distribute presents among them with an unstinted hand. Being well satisfied with their cordial reception, the assembled warriors soon departed with minds at ease.[3]

If the situation in regard to the Indians was felt to be critical by the officers in East Florida—and it undoubtedly was—the English government also felt some trepidation about the attitude the red men in that province would assume when they should learn of the intended cession of this region to Spain. Accordingly, in February, 1783, orders were sent from Whitehall to Colonel Brown to have all the officers of his department withdraw with the traders from the Indian country and to distribute to its denizens all presents remaining in the stores at St. Augustine.[4] This looked as though Great Britain regarded her account with

1. *Report on the Am. Mss. in the Roy. Inst. of G. Brit.*, *III.* 325, 334
2. *Ibid.*, 277, 316, 322.
3. *Ibid.*, 325, 326, 334, 367.
4. *Ibid.*, 358.

the Florida Indians as virtually closed. That the Indians themselves did not so regard it is shown by General McArthur's comments concerning them in a letter to Carleton of May 19, 1783. He wrote: "The minds of these people appear as much agitated as those of the loyalists on the eve of a third evacuation; and however chimerical it may appear to us, they have very seriously proposed to abandon their country and accompany us, having made all the world their enemies by their attachment to us." [1]

Colonel Brown, who wrote to the same effect, also testified to the past faithfulness of his proteges, and asked for vessels to remove them. He received assurance that those who persevered in their demand would be furnished with conveyance to the Bahamas; but they were to be dissuaded, if possible, on the score that the islands were not a suitable place for them. This was more easily said than done, for after an interval of several months, McArthur still felt constrained to write (September 13, 1783) of his apprehensions that many of the Indians would insist on accompanying him to the Bahamas. [2]

The provincial regiments in East Florida did not accept as readily the prospect of their removal. This was largely due to the insinuations that reached them through irresponsible persons, namely, that they were to be sent off to the East and West Indies without their consent. The spread of these rumors almost produced a mutiny among the troops, and they demanded their discharge. However, they were promptly reduced to obedience, and the ringleaders were punished. Later, they were assured that there was no intention of deporting them, and that every man was to have the liberty of going where he pleased, indeed, of placing himself under the rule of Spain or the United States, if he chose. [3]

II. The Loyalists in West Florida

West Florida was out of range of the swarms of provincial troops, refugees, and negroes sent down to her sister province; but she was by no means devoid of loyal inhabitants, and she received a considerable accession of incorporated loyalists and

1. *Report on the Am. Mss. in the Roy. Inst. of G. Brit.*, *IV*, 89.
2. *Ibid.*
3. *Ibid*, 90, 165.

other refugees from the colonies farther north. Certain planters of the province presented a petition to the House of Commons in March, 1787, in which they stated that many of their fellow colonials had joined the King's troops, while the refugees in West Florida had formed themselves into provincial corps and faced the dangers of the field.[1] Among these refugees was Captain Richard Peavis, who after engaging four hundred men for service in the peninsula was forced to flee, he tells us, from the vicinity of Charleston to Pensacola, taking with him six companions. In 1777, he was commissioned a captain in the West Florida Loyalists by Colonel Stuart, and was constantly employed thereafter until he settled on St. John's River, East Florida, in 1783.[2] Doubtless, the corps which Captain Peavis joined was that officially styled the West Florida Loyal Refugees organized by Colonel Charles Stuart, the superintendent of Indian affairs at Pensacola, and disbanded at the end of November, 1779, by Major General John Campbell, who was in command in the province.[3] In the following year, however, General Campbell found it expedient to enroll a new corps known as the West Florida Royal Foresters. This troop remained in service until its reduction, August 15, 1782. Evidently, the Foresters were organized about the time the Spanish attack on Pensacola was expected, which was as early as May, 1780.[4] That the attack did not take place at this time was partly due, Campbell thought, to the presence of a large body of Indians, which had been assembled in the town for its protection.[5]

But the defense of West Florida did not fall alone upon the Indians and the Royal Foresters. Campbell had under his command other forces, including the third battalion of the Sixtieth Regiment, the third regiment of the Waldeck troops, and the United Corps of Pennsylvania and Maryland Loyalists—the last numbering two hundred and sixty-seven men, with Lieutenant-Colonel William Allen at their head. He also had a company of Military Batteaux men, probably loyalists, under Captain Miller.[6]

1. *Journals of the House of Commons*, 27 Geo. III, *Vol. XLII*, 551, 552.
2. *Report of the Bureau of Archives, Ont.*, Pt. I, 190, 191.
3. *Report on the Am. Mss. in the Roy. Inst. of G. Brit.*, II, 159, 160.
4. *Ibid., IV*, 445.
5. *Ibid., II*, 121, 122.
6. *Ibid., III*, 169, 170.

According to General Campbell, these troops had been left without an adequate supply of cannon and artillery stores; but they nevertheless held out for nearly two months after Don Galves and his Spanish fleet entered the harbor of Pensacola. When, however, a well directed shot from the blockading force exploded the powder magazine, the place capitulated, May 9, 1781.[1]

What became of the loyalists of West Florida at this time is difficult to discover. We are told that part of the garrison of Pensacola was sent to New York;[2] and we have information of the arrival in London of a party of the Maryland and Pennsylvania Loyalists under the command of Lieutenant Inglis. This party was made up of invalids who desired admission to the military hospital at Chelsea and set sail from Pensacola for that destination in the early months of 1780.[3] Before the evacuation of the New York, nearly three and a half years later, the larger part of the Maryland Loyalists sailed in the ship *Martha* with the fall fleet for the Bay of Fundy to settle in Nova Scotia; but their vessel was wrecked, late in September, 1783, off Tusket River, and over one hundred lives were lost. "It is recorded," says Paul Leicester Ford, "that the troop stood drawn up in company order, while the women and children were ordered into the boats, and the few survivors among the men were chiefly saved by clinging to wreckage."[4] In an undated list of persons who embarked for Nova Scotia, probably aboard the fated transport, we find the names of Lieutenant-Colonel James Chalmers, organizer of the troop, and Lieutenant-Colonel William Allen of the Pennsylvania Loyalists.[5] Captain Adam Chrystie of the Foresters was still in New York City, November 3, when he signed a petition for a grant of land in Nova Scotia.[6] Captain Richard Peavis of the West Florida Refugees found himself doomed to leave his place of settlement on the St. John's River, East Florida, and betook

1. *Report on the Am. Mss. in the Roy. Inst. of G. Brit.*, II, 281, 286, 514, 515.
2. *Orderly Book of the "Maryland Loyalists Regiment,"* 12, n.
3. *Report on the Am. Mss. in the Roy. Inst. of G. Brit.*, II, 109, 110, 150.
4. *Orderly Book of the "Maryland Loyalists Regiment,"* 11; *Report on the Am. Mss. in the Roy. Inst. of G. Brit.*, IV, 380, 409, 420, 440.
5. *Report on the Am. Mss. in the Roy. Inst. of G. Brit.*, IV, 479, 105.
6. *Ibid.*, IV, 443.

himself to the Island of Abaco in the Bahamas.¹ A few others from West Florida, with their slaves, arrived in Jamaica during the summer of 1783, settling chiefly in Kingston, according to the parish records of that island. While these are only scattered instances, they serve to illustrate the vicissitudes of the loyalists of West Florida after the conquest of that province by Spain.

III. The Emigration of Loyalists to Jamaica

East Florida escaped subjugation by the Spaniards, but nevertheless shared the fate of the adjoining district when England made peace with Spain. By the treaty of Versailles, the latter country gained both provinces, but the loyalists preferred the hardships of another removal rather than submit to Spanish rule. During the earlier years of the Revolution, refugees had taken shelter under the British flag in Jamaica and the Bahamas. In October, 1775, one of the London papers gave currency to the item that several American families had arrived in Jamaica with their effects "on account of troubles in their own country." ² When Sir James Wright, governor of Georgia, fled to England in March, 1776, a considerable number of Georgia loyalists took their departure to the West Indies and Bahamas. It is true that some of these returned after Governor Wright resumed his office in the spring of 1777, but not all of them did so. ³

When in July, 1782, Savannah was evacuated, less than half of the 7,000 persons who withdrew from that port went to East Florida; Governor Wright, with some of the officers, civil and military, and part of the garrison, disembarked at Charleston; Brigadier-General Alured Clark and part of the British regulars went to New York; and the remainder—described as inhabitants and their effects—sailed to Jamaica under convoy of the frigate *Zebra*. ⁴ Doubtless, these effects were mostly slaves, for Mr. Wright and some of his fellow loyalists had no less than two thousand for shipment to the island. The Governor explained afterwards that he considered Jamaica the best market for his

1. *Report of the Bureau of Archives, Ont., Pt., I,* 190, 191.
2. Lloyd's *Evening Post*, Oct. 4-6, 1775.
3. *Report of the Bureau of Archives, Ont., Pt. II,* 1305; Audit Office Claims, IV, Public Records Office, London.
4. *Report on the Am. Mss. in the Roy. Inst. of G. Brit., III,* 65, 126.

negroes, and that they were in danger of being stolen at Savannah.[1] Probably, much more of the same kind of property was transported to the same destination. At any rate, Bridges tells us in his *Annals of Jamaica*[2] that the island gained nearly 5,000, besides four hundred white families, by the evacuation of Savannah.

When, in December, 1782, Charleston was surrendered to the Americans, 3,891 persons embarked for Jamaica, of whom 1,278 were whites and 2,613 were blacks. At the same time, twenty whites and three hundred and fifty blacks sailed for St. Lucia. It will be remembered that the number carried from Charleston to East Florida was almost equal to that destined for Jamaica. Of the remainder, two hundred and forty sailed for New York, four hundred and seventy, for Halifax, and three hundred and twentyfour, for England.[3]

What the result of the exodus from East Florida may have been for Jamaica and the other West Indies is not clear. At the end of July, 1782, some of the Georgia refugees at St. Augustine memoralized Carleton, informing him that there were at least 4000 people of both races from their colony in their neighborhood, and that they regarded the West Indies as the only region where they could employ their slaves to any advantage.[4] But we have no means of ascertaining how many of these people found their way to the desired destination. The same uncertainty appertains to the various families in New York City who were seeking conveyance to these islands during the years 1782 and 1783.[5] That a considerable proportion of them succeeded in reaching their goal admits of little doubt. Sabine gives several instances of Massachusetts Tories who settled in Antigua and St. Christophers.[6] Near the close of May, 1783, eighty-five persons registered at St. Augustine to go to Jamaica, and a ship with these refugees,

1. *Report on the Am. Mss. in the Roy. Inst. of G. Brit.*, *III*, 28; *Report of the Bureau of Archives, Ont.*, Pt. II ,18c6.
2. P. 190.
3. *South Carolina Historical Magazine*, Jan., 1910, 26.
4. *Report on Am. Mss. in the Roy Inst. of G. Brit.*, *III*, 45.
5. *Ibid.*, *III* 230, 260, 363, 365; *IV*, 161, 228, 234, 374, 399, 480; *Second Report of the Bureau of Archives, Ont.*, Pt. II, 914, 929, 1132, 1133.
6. *American Loyalists*, 1847, 551, 587, 221.

and probably others, sailed from that place for the island named about the twenty-fifth of the following month.[1]

Some of the new settlers in Jamaica came also from Honduras and the Mosquito Shore, where the British had colonies engaged in cutting logwood and mahogany. The Spanish had long regarded these people as intruders in Central America, and during the later years of the Revolution attacked them with such persistence as to drive them out.[2] Their certificates of loyalty are still to be found among the official records of their chosen retreat, and show that they arrived at various times during the year 1783, some being accompanied by their slaves. Their numbers were sufficiently large to cause them to be mentioned in certain acts passed by the Assembly of Jamaica in 1783 and 1784.[3] The certificates also bear testimony to the fact that loyalists continued to come to this island down to 1788 from both Northern and Southern states, albeit in very small numbers. Doubtless, Jamaica profited also by the dispersion of the 10,000 refugees who were sent from New York to Shelburne, Nova Scotia, in the spring and fall of 1783. This dispersion took place during the years from 1785 to 1788, inclusive; and we are told by Mr. T. Watson Smith, author of "*The Loyalists at Shelburne*," a paper showing careful and extensive investigation, that numbers of these exiles found their way not only to the Canadas and Great Britain, but also to the West Indies.[4] The above facts help to explain the remarkable increase in population of Jamaica between the years 1775 and 1787. The census for the former year showed 18,500 whites, 3,700 free colored people, and 190,914 slaves; while for the latter year the figures are 30,000 whites, 10,000 free colored people, and 250,000 slaves.[5] By 1785 the number of slaves had already reached from 220,000 to 240,000.[6]

IV. The Loyalists in the Bahamas

During the greater part of the War—if we may trust our evidence—the Bahamas benefitted but little by the misfortunes

1. *Report on the Am. Mss. in the Roy. Inst. of G. Brit.*, IV, 92, 93.
2. Morris, *The Colony of British Honduras*.
3. *Acts of the Assembly of Jamaica, 1778-1783*, 337; *1784-1791*, 32.
4. *Collections of the Nova Scotia Historical Society, 1787-8*, 57, 63, 65, 85, 86, 88.
5. Gardner, *History of Jamaica*, 221.
6. Martin, *History of the West Indies*, I, 90.

of the American refugees. Moreover, early in May, 1782, they had the mishap to fall, like West Florida, into the hands of Spain. But Spain was not able to keep them long, for in April, 1783, Major Andrew DeVeaux, a provincial officer of South Carolina, left St. Augustine with "a handful of ragged militia and five privateers" to recover New Providence. In this he succeeded, despite the presence of five hundred Spaniards, seventy pieces of cannon, and six galleys. This was the last episode of the Revolutionary War, which thus closed with a British victory won by American loyalists acting on their own motion. The irony of the affair is enhanced by the circumstance that Deveaux's success had been anticipated nine days before by England's treaty with Spain, the fifth article of which restored the Bahama Islands to Great Britain.[1] At the same time, the treaty deprived the loyalists of the Floridas as a place of refuge, for it surrendered them to the Spanish King The sole consolation of the Southern loyalists was that the ill wind that swept them from their last retreat on the mainland was to bear them to the neighboring islands, including the Bahamas.

The first intimation of the intended evacuation of East Florida reached Governor Tonyn as early as June, 1782, and caused him much surprise and sorrow; while it produced nothing less than consternation among the loyalists, both old inhabitants and refugees. The Assembly of Georgia remonstrated against the proposal, recommending that the territory be kept as an asylum for the loyalists. The Assembly of East Florida asked for some defense in case the troops should be withdrawn, and resolved to stand by the Governor in preserving the allegiance of the province. Tonyn took up with Carleton the question of the removal of the garrison from St. Augustine, and secured his consent to a delay. He was thus encouraged to hope that the King would find a way of retaining the province permanently, and, doubtless, this hope was still further encouraged by Carleton's instructions to grant lands free of quit rent to officers and soldiers desirous of settling in East Florida on the establishment of peace.[2]

1. *Report on the Am. Mss. in the Roy. Inst. of G. Brit.*, *IV*, vi, vii, 93, 128, 169, 247, 293, 351.
2. *Ibid.*, *II*, 513, 520, 527, 528, 529, 530, 531, 546; *III*, 19, 417.

However, the publication of the peace rudely destroyed any such expectations. It only left the loyalists a choice between living under Spanish rule, which they greatly dreaded, and preserving their fealty by withdrawing to some British possession. By the eighth article of the treaty, those subjects of England who proposed to remove were allowed eighteen months in which to collect their debts, sell their property, and leave the country. Tonyn received orders to coöperate with McArthur in effecting the evacuation in conformity with this provision, and made proclamation accordingly.[1] Judging by the official correspondence that has come down to us, these measures did not produce a marked effect at once. We have already seen that a single ship was sufficient to carry those who embarked at St. Augustine near the end of June, 1783, for Jamaica. It may be added that two vessels sufficed for those taking passage for England, and that while ninety signed to go to New Providence, no reference is made to their departure at this time.[2] This disinclination on the part of the loyalists to proceed to the Bahamas was due to a lack of information about the conditions obtaining there. Hence, some of the intending settlers of New Providence went to find out what they could about these conditions, and were soon followed by Lieutenant Wilson, of the Engineers, who was officially dispatched from St. Augustine for the same purpose. The report made by the former was not very favorable, and is embodied in a letter of McArthur of September 7: it represented that the soil was rocky and that there were "no tracts of land contiguous where any considerable number of negroes could be employed." On Wilson's return, he found instructions from Robert Morse, chief engineer at New York, extending his tour of inspection to all of the Bahamas, evidently in compliance with a request of Carleton, who had recommended to the British goverment that any lands ungranted or escheated in the islands be given free of expense to those loyalists who had lost their property through their allegiance, and should choose the Bahamas as a place of settlement.[3] Lieutenant Wilson was therefore sent back to the

1. *Report on the Am. Mss. in the Roy. Inst. of G. Brit.*, IV, 57, 93.
2. *Ibid.*, IV, 92, 93.
3. *Ibid.*, IV, 158, 204, 233, 340, vii, 224, 233, 247, 248, 351.

islands, and gathered the information for an extended report that proved to be more reassuring than that of the prospective settlers in New Providence.

Indeed, this report left little doubt concerning the availability of the Bahamas for colonization by the refugees. It ascribed the uncultivated condition of the islands to the indolence of the inhabitants, who contented themselves, it declared, with whatever nature produced by her unaided efforts. They took no trouble to clear the land, but planted small patches of Guinea corn, yams, and sugar cane, which they left without futher care until the crop was ready to be gathered. It asserted that pineapples, oranges, lemons, limes, cocoa, and other fruits common to the West Indies would readily grow in the Bahamas, and maintained that the soil had never been put to a fair test, such as it would now be subjected to by the new settlers. It did not attempt to conceal the fact that the islands were rocky and the surface rough, but called attention to the three kinds of soil existing there, one adapted to the growth of cotton, another to the raising of vegetables of all kinds, and the third to the production of Guineacorn. [1]

Reassuring as this report proved to be, it came too late to start the movement of the loyalists from Florida to the Bahamas. The event that gave the impetus to this movement was the arrival of some government transports and victuallers at St. Augustine on September 12, 1783. By this time many of the loyalists had become convinced that they could no longer stand on the order of their going, but must go at once. Two days later a number of them applied to McArthur for conveyance to the islands for themselves and their negroes.[2] Unfortunately, we are left in ignorance as to the success or failure of their application. But as Lieutenant-Colonel Brown and most of his regiment of East Florida Rangers, together with a few of the men of the North and South Carolina regiments, made their decision in favor of the Bahamas at this time, it is highly probable that conveyance was supplied to all those desiring it. Of the North Carolina corps, however,

1. Stark, *History and Guide to the Bahama Islands*, 172, 173.
2. *Report on the Am. Mss. in the Roy. Inst. of G. Brit.*, IV, 351, 356.

more than half asked for passage to Nova Scotia, while nearly two-thirds of the South Carolina corps chose to be discharged from service in St. Augustine.[1] Although we catch but few glimpses of what was taking place in East Florida during the remainder of the time allowed for its evacuation, we can scarcely doubt that parties of varying size, some in small vessels supplied by themselves, were embarking from time to time for the Bahamas and the neighboring islands. This exodus was encouraged not only by Wilson's report, and by the means of transportation provided by the Crown, but also by the favorable conditions offered to those who wished to settle in the archipelago. According to instructions issued to Lieutenant-Governor Powell, September 10, 1784, he was to grant unoccupied lands in the Bahamas as follows: "To every head of a family, forty acres, and to every white or black man, woman or child in a family, twenty acres, at an annual quit rent of 2s. per hundred acres. But in the case of the Loyalist refugees from the continent such lands were to be delivered free of charges, and were to be exempted from the burden of the quit rents for ten years from the date of making the grants." These instructions were issued none too soon, for only fifteen days afterwards a number of transports and ordinance vessels arrived at Nassau with the garrison and military stores of St. Augustine. With this fleet came McArthur, whom Carleton had placed in command of the Bahamas for the time being. Within a few days there arrived also "seven ships and two brigs crowded with refugees." We are told that the stream of loyalists continued to pour into the islands during the early months of the following year, Spain having extended by four months the period allowed for the withdrawal of British subjects from Florida. Even this concession proved barely sufficient, for Governor Tonyn appropriated a few days of grace by making announcement that the last transport would leave the port of St. Mary's River, on March 1, 1785. He advised all persons of English blood to leave East Florida for the Bahamas before the Spanish governor took possession.[2]

1. *Report on the Am. Mss. in the Roy. Inst. of G. Brit.*, IV, 351.
2. Geographical Society of Baltimore, *The Bahama Islands*, 424; Northcroft, *Sketches of Summerland*, 281; Campbell, *Historical Sketches of Colonial Florida*, 142; Fairbanks, *History of Florida*, 239.

But East Florida was not the only important source of the multitudes coming to settle in the Bahama Islands during our period. From New York City, Carleton sent more than 1,400 persons, who had associated themselves to colonize the Island of Abaco. On August 10, 1783, Brook Watson, commissary-general at New York, reported that most of this party—or, in his own words, "near a thousand souls"—were ready to embark. He saw to it that they were supplied with provisions sufficient to serve them for six months after their arrival, and recommended Phillip Dumaresq, a Boston loyalist, as commissary to accompany them and distribute the provisions. This recommendation was carried into effect, and Dumaresq probably sailed with the first contingent, which left New York sometime before August 22. Other refugees embarked at the same time for Cat Island. Carleton now shipped provisions for an additional six months, and instructed McArthur to do everything in his power for the exiles. During the month of October, two additional contingents of the associators got ready to sail, one of those numbering five hundred and nine persons. All told, 1,458 loyalists embarked at New York for Abaco, according to an official return of the Commissary-General, dated two days before the British troops evacuated that port.[1] This number does not include eight companies of militia sent from New York to the Bahamas in October 1783.[2] That Abaco derived part of its settlers from East Florida is indicated by a memorial, addressed to Carleton in June of the year just named, by some of the New York associators. This memorial stated that many persons from St. Augustine were expected to join the new colony, and another memorial, published in New York about the same time, announced more explicitly that the number of loyal inhabitants of East Florida who had actually engaged to take part in the settlement of Abaco was upwards of 1,500.[3] On October 21, Carleton communicated to Major-General Edward Mathew, commandant of the British West Indies, that he expected adherents of the Crown to remove from East Florida to the Bahamas during the following winter, and ordered him to send six months provisions for 2,000 men to

1. *Report on the Am. Mss. in the Roy. Inst. of G. Brit.*, IV, 470, 271, 272, 283, 407, 437, x.
2. *Ibid.*, 398.
3. *Report on the Am. Mss. in the Roy. Inst. of G. Brit.*, IV, 188· *Manual of the Corporation of the City of New York, 1870*, 791.

New Providence, in addition to the supplies that had been already sent from New York. He hoped thus to provide a quantity sufficient to subsist the new settlers until they should be able to raise their own produce.[1]

It is difficult to estimate the increase in population of the Bahamas due to the immigration of the loyalists. Bryan Edwards, writing at the beginning of the nineteenth century, does not attempt it, but contents himself with telling us that the inhabitants who in 1773 numbered 2,052 whites and 2,241 blacks were "considerably augmented" by the emigrants from North America.[2] Northcroft, writing in 1900, is more positive: he states that before the emigration there were only 1,750 white people in the colony and 2,300 colored; but that the influx of refugees raised the number of the former to 3,500 and the latter to 6,500.[3] Dr. Wright, who investigated the subject in 1905, seems to accept these figures.[4] But, according to a census of 1782, in which seven of the islands are named, the total number of inhabitants was 4,002, less then one quarter being negroes. In the light of the evidence presented in this paper, it seems safe to say that the Bahama Islands gained between 6,000 and 7,000 inhabitants of both races from June, 1783, to April, 1785.

One of those who came to the Bahamas later than most of the others loyalists was Colonel David Fanning of North Carolina, who received his commission in the Loyal Militia of Randolph and Chatham Counties in July, 1781.[5] It is true that Colonel Fanning remained only a short time in the islands; but his adventures between the evacuation of Charleston and his arrival at Nassau, serve to illustrate vividly the vicissitudes of the Southern refugees during this trying period. At the end of September, 1782, Fanning and his wife were at Charleston, where the shipping was ready for those desiring to embark for St.

1. *Report on the Am. Mss. in the Roy. Inst. of G. Brit.*, IV, 420, 421.
2. *History of the West Indies*, II, 199, 200; Lucas, *Historical Geography of the British Colonies*, II, 80, n.
3. *Sketches in Summerland*, 282.
4. *History of the Bahama Islands*, 425.
5. *Fanning's Narrative*, 1908, 17; *Report of the Bureau of Archives Ont.*, Pt., I, 241

Augustine. Many loyalists had previously signed to go under his direction to East Florida. Accordingly, he ordered them to embark, and, on November 6, went on board the transport *New Blessing*, whose name doubtless seemed something of a mockery before that vessel sailed eight days later. On November 17, the convoy cast anchor off the Florida coast, and there laid eight days more before its weary passengers could go ashore. After another but briefer delay, Fanning was able to get his effects landed at a point about twenty-seven miles from St. Augustine on the Matangeys, where he thought of settling. Becoming dissatisfied there, he went next to a more distant locality on the Halifax River to established a plantation, for which he had a supply of negroes.

In February, 1783, having met Major Deveaux, who was collecting volunteers for his expedition to capture New Providence, Colonel Fanning agreed to join him, and raised thirty men for the purpose; but through some oversight was left behind. Later, several of the Colonel's slaves took sick and died, thereby destroying his hopes of establishing a plantation. He, therefore, moved into St. Augustine, but only to fall desperately ill himself. Shortly after his recovery from this sickness, the news of the peace reached East Florida, and the evacuation of that province was ordered. At the same time, the ships came that were to carry the provincial troops to Nova Scotia; but Fanning's personal property was still in the country, and he had not yet decided where he wished to go. Before settling this point, he visited the Mosquito Shore, and received from its inhabitants a petition addressed to Governor Tonyn, under date of January 24, 1784. This petition asked for a schooner to transport the inhabitants to East Florida before the intended surrender of that province, as the petitioners desired to leave with the other loyalists. Fanning delivered this message to the Governor, and appears to have carried back in person the latter's reply, namely, that the inhabitants must get to the shipping as best as they could, inasmuch as there were no government vessels available to send for them. In a speech that Fanning made to these people, he declared that the loyalists had been sacrificed to the indignation of their enemies, and that nothing was to be expected of Great Britain. He, therefore, advised his hearers to throw themselves on the mercy of the Spaniards, and announced his own intention of betaking himself to the farthest limits of West Florida, in order to settle "at or near Fort Notches [Natchez] on the Mississippi River."

That this was not idle talk is shown by the fact that Colonel Fanning set out, March 20, 1784, from St. Augustine, with seven families, his wife, and two negroes, all in open boats, for the Mississippi country. After sailing one hundred and sixty miles, he lost sight of his companions, and never saw them afterwards, although he waited for them twelve days, he tells us, at "Scibersken." From that point, he journeyed to Key West, where he was detained by a gale for more than a fortnight. There he met a Spanish schooner, and was warned that his boat was too small for the voyage he was undertaking, and that he stood a poor chance of escaping death at the hands of the Indians. Thereupon, he sailed back to one of the other keys, where he found an Italian skipper from New Providence, engaged in catching turtles. Fanning discovered this man to be untrustworthy and grasping, but, having no other alternative, engaged passage with him at an exorbitant price. Fortunately, however, the arrival of several other seaman from the Bahamas, on July 12, enabled Colonel and Mrs. Fanning to make the voyage to New Providence with a captain who showed them every attention. Landing at Nassau, the Fannings remained there only twenty days, and then sailed for New Brunswick, where they cast anchor, September 23, 1784. They departed a month later for Halifax, Nova Scotia, with a view to obtaining land for settlement.[1]

Abaco, which probably received a greater share of the immigrants than any of the other Bahamas, is the largest island of the group, and one of the most fertile. Philip Dumaresq, who remained there as commissary for more than a year and a half, gives some particulars regarding the island, which enable us to identify it with Great Abaco: the length of the island, he says, is about a hundred miles, and in shape it "forms an elbow." He found the climate delightful, but noted that the soil was so shallow that in a dry season the sun heated the rock underneath and burned up any vegetables that had been planted. He also recorded

1. *Flanning's Narrative*, 1908, 37-46.

that an unusual drought had prevailed almost from the time the loyalists had arrived there. He wrote that Guinea corn, potatoes, yams, turnips, and other garden produce would grow very well, together with such fruits as oranges, limes, and plantains (bananas), and that cotton would thrive; but he complained that the settlers were all poor, had not the strength to do much, and that he had seen no fresh meat, except pork, since his arrival. However, poultry, he said, could be raised in plenty. The abundance of wild grapes convinced him that good wines might be produced, and he was told that indigo could be cultivated successfully. He and his family did not find the people of Abaco at all congenial, and he speaks of them in no complimentary terms in the letter to his father-in-law, Dr. Sylvester Gardiner, the Boston loyalist, from which we glean our informant's impressions of the island and its occupants; on the other hand, the Commissary had nothing but good words for the treatment accorded him by John Maxwell, governor of the Bahamas, and General McArthur. These gentlemen, he testified, treated him only with the greatest politeness, and the former appointed him a magistrate in order, he declared, to keep him from being "insulted by the Abaco Blackguards."[1]

If, however, Governor Maxwell showed himself kindly disposed towards this lone loyalist officer, he yet exhibited an unmistakable prejudice, which he shared with the older inhabitants, towards the new element in the colony. The coming of the loyalists thus brought with it factional feeling—feeling that grew so pronounced ere long as to lead the new settlers to disavow openly any responsibility for an address of regret presented to the Governor when he surrendered his office, and returned to England in the summer of 1785. The Americans promptly became the party of opposition to the existing government in the islands: they criticized the administration, accused Governor Maxwell of attempting to withold from them the right of trial by jury, and of other conduct which they characterized as tyrannical. They also found fault with some of the laws, on the ground that they were repugnant to those of the mother country, and they demanded reform. The elections of 1785 gave the loyalists some

1. The Gardiner, Whipple, and Allen Letters, Vol. II, 49. (In the Library of the Massachusetts Historical Society, in Boston.)

25

members in the House of Assembly, but the native population was still in control there; and when several members, who favored the new party, withdrew from the House and persisted in absenting themselves against the House's orders, they were declared to be no longer eligible to seats in that body. The loyalists sent a petition to the Assembly asking for its dissolution, which, after being read, was handed over to the common hangman to be burned before the door of the House.

By the latter part of 1786, the Americans had become the stronger party in the Bahamas; but the Earl of Dunmore, who succeeded to the governorship at this time, pursued the same policy as his predecessor. He received petitions from New Providence, Abaco, Exuma, and Cat Island, again praying that the Assembly be dissolved; but, as he declined to accede to them, that body lasted about eight years longer, or until the end of Dunmore's administration. Then, finally, an act was passed that limited the life of a legislature to seven years.

Up to 1787, the title of the lands of the Bahamas had been vested in the Lords Proprietors of the islands. Now, however, the proprietary rights of these gentlemen passed to the Crown "on the payment of £2,000 to each of them." Henceforth, the King would exercise the rights of granting lands and collecting quit rents, although this was to be with less success, insofar as the quit rents were concerned, then under the Lords Proprietors.[1]

Besides affecting political conditions in the colony, the influx of the loyalists had a marked effect upon the commercial, agricultural, and social conditions of the archipelago. By 1800 the town of Nassau alone had a population—a little more than 3,000—equal to the whole population of the only islands inhabited thirty years before, namely, New Providence, Eleuthera, and Harbor Island. The exports of Nassau are said to have amounted only to £5,200 for the years 1773 and 1774, and her imports to £3,600 for the same period; while for 1786 and 1787 the former had increased in value to £5,800, exclusive of the large amount of bullion exported, and the latter to £136,360. McKinnen, who made a tour of the Bahamas in 1802 and 1803, reports that six square-rigged vessels were seen at one time in Nassau harbor laden

1. Fiske, *The West Indies.* 125; Geographical Society of Baltimore, *The Bahama Islands*, 426.

with cotton for London, and tells us that during many years previous the exports of this commodity amounted to several hundred tons per annum. He also notes that the town was frequently visited while he remained there by African slave-ships, some of which disposed of their cargoes on the island. The principal trade of Nassau, McKinnen says, was carried on with England, the southern islands in the West Indies, and the United States, whence it derived continual supplies of live stock and provisions.[1] The same authority states that the exports from the islands included salt, turtles, mahogany, dye and other woods and barks. Wrecking was also a source of considerable income, since wrecks were continually occurring among the Bahamas.[2]

Agriculture, even more than commerce, was given a new impetus by the American refugees, many of whom were planters from the South, accompanied by a considerable number of their slaves. It did not take these experienced cotton raisers long to clear lands and plant their crops. "It is said that fifteen years after their arrival, forty plantations, with between 2,000 and 3,000 acres in cotton fields, had been established on Crooked Island alone, and that on Long Island, which was settled at an earlier date, and which had been more extensively improved, there were in 1783 nearly 4,000 acres in cultivation. The combined yield from Long Island and Exuma for one year was estimated at over 600 tons." McKinnen found that the planters—most of whom came from Georgia, according to his account—had brought with them different varieties of seed, especially the Persian, but that Anguilla cotton was being more generally cultivated at the time of his visit. It was customary to assign not more than four acres of Persian plants to each working slave, while five or six acres formed the usual allotment on the plantations where the Anguilla cotton was being grown. The best crops were secured from the higher lands, and amounted to one-half or three-fourths of a ton of clean lint for each working slave on some estates, although the average yield was about one-sixth of a ton or less. Another crop

1. Geographical Society of Baltimore, *The Bahama Islands*, 148; McKinnen, *Tour Through the British West Indies*, 216, 217; Northcroft, *Sketches of Summerland*, 282; McKinnen, *Tour Through the British West Indies*, 218, 219.

2. Geographical Society of Baltimore, *The Bahama Islands*, 149.

that was universally cultivated was Guinea corn. The production of cotton, however, was not destined to be permanently successful. When McKinnen visited the islands in 1802-1803, he found the plantations on Crooked Island for the most part deserted, and the proprietors generally despondent over the agricultural outlook. Mr. Charles N. Mooney of the United States Bureau of Soils, who has thoroughly investigated this subject, thinks that the same conditions probably prevailed in all the other islands, and proceeds to explain that the failure of cotton was due chiefly to the attacks of insects, but that other causes were also operative, as disclosed by a committee of planters who looked into the matter at the time. This committee reported as additional causes for the failure of cotton growing, "the use of land unsuited to its culture, the injudicious and wasteful methods of clearing the land, and the exhaustion of the soil by unremitted tillage." The result appears to have been a marked decline in the production of cotton after the year 1805, together with a decrease in the value of land and slaves.[1] These conditions led inevitably to the emigration of some of the planters with their negroes before the exportation of slaves from the British colonies was prohibited, and to attempts at securing the right to emigrate with them after the slave trade was abolished in 1807. These conditions serve to explain the return to Florida of a body of loyalists who formed a settlement at New Smyrna, although they soon abandoned this place to seek homes in the States on account of the distasteful policy of the Spanish administration.[2] The news of the activity of the opponents of slavery in England, which did not reach the Bahamas until 1815, must have had a further demoralizing effect upon cotton culture in the islands; and when slavery was abolished in 1834 cotton ceased to be an important crop. We are told that the fine estates that had been built up were now deserted and that the owners either moved to Nassau or left the islands altogether.[3] When emancipation was declared the Bahama slave owners received £128,296 for their negroes, or £12, 14s, 4d, per head. This was a comparatively low figure,

1. Geographical Society of Baltimore, *The Bahama Islands*, 148, 149; McKinnen. *Tour Through the British West Indies*, 183; Geographical Society of Baltimore, *The Bahama Islands*, 426, 552.
2. Fairbanks, *History of Florida*, 244.
3. Geographical Society of Baltimore, *The Bahama Islands*, 149, 429.

considering the reimbursements of other colonies; but this fact may possibly be regarded as proof that slave labor was not very remunerative in the Bahamas.[1]

The presence of the American refugees affected more or less the social conditions in the Bahamas, for the newcomers soon outnumbered the older inhabitants, and they introduced their own conceptions of plantation life and of the relations of master and slave. Many of the new whites were persons of energy, and we have McKinnen's word for it that the blacks in general possessed "more spirit and execution" than those in the southern parts of the West Indies. The planters assigned the various tasks to their negroes, "daily and individually" according to their strength; and if the latter were so diligent as to have finished their labors at an early hour, the rest of the day was allowed them for amusement or their private concerns. Another feature that tended to soften the system of slavery in the islands was the absence of the overseer from most of the estates. The master usually acted as his own superintendent; and it rarely happened, therefore, according to McKinnen, that the negroes were so much subject to the discipline of the whip as was the case where the gangs were large, and the direction of them was entrusted to agents or overseers. It was, nevertheless, true that some planters were brutal, that female slaves as well as males were sometimes flogged, and that masters "had the right practically to punish their slaves at their own discretion," without being held accountable for their acts of cruelty.[2]

The immigration to the Bahamas probably trebled the number of blacks, and raised the relative majority of blacks over whites by more than twenty per cent. It is not surprising, therefore, that the stringency of the laws regulating slaves should have been increased. The sentiments and fears of the ruling class, which arose out of the changed situation, appear in the legislation enacted by the General Assembly of the colony in 1784. This legislation provided for the punishment of assault on a white by a slave with death; it provided that other abuse of a white person

1. Northcroft, *Sketches of Summerland*, 292.
2. Edwards, *West Indies*, Vol. IV, Ap., 358; Northcroft, *Sketches of Summerland*, 285.

should be atoned for by a fine of £15, or by corporal punishment, not limited in amount or character; it provided that "whites could disarm not only slaves but also free coloured persons whom they found at large with arms in their hands;" it imposed a tax of £90 on any one manumitting a bondman, and gave validity to the evidence of slaves against manumitted persons in all trials for capital or criminal offenses; while against white persons only Christian negroes, mulattos, mustees, or Indians were allowed to testify at all, and they only in suits for debt.[1]

In 1796 it was enacted that slave owners should endeavor to instruct their slaves in the Christian religion, and have those baptized who could be made sensible of a Deity and of the Christian faith; but as there was only one clergyman in the entire colony at that time it is not likely that many slaves were baptized.[2]

Inasmuch as planters were sometimes annoyed by the escape of their slaves, it was customary to offer private rewards for the return of the runaways. We are told that hardly an issue of the *Bahama Gazette* appeared in 1794 and 1795 that did not give notice of the escape of a fugitive. At length an epidemic of escapes into the interior occurred in the small island of New Providence, and a law was passed ordering the registration of all free negroes, mulattoes, mustees, and Indians, and providing that if at any time five or more runaways were reported, free negroes might be sent in pursuit of them. Colored freemen were promised rewards for the arrest and delivery of runaways, and were allowed to kill a fugitive slave, if necessary, in order to defend themselves from his attack.[3]

Slaves were excluded from service in the local militia. So, also, were free blacks until the year 1804. After that time, prejudice served as a sufficient bar against the exercise of this right until after emancipation was declared. Much the same restrictions held in regard to jury service by negroes during the same period.[4]

By a statute of 1805, the trial of all suits relating to the freedom of slaves was confined to the highest tribunal in the colony,

1. Geographical Society of Baltimore, *The Bahama Islands*, 449, 450, 451, 456; Northcroft, *Sketches in Summerland*, 288.
2. Northcroft, *Sketches in Summerland*, 288.
3. Geographical Society of Baltimore, *The Bahama Islands*, 453.
4. *Ibid.*, 448.

namely, the General Court. As that body sat only in the island of New Providence, it was necessary to provide that in the case of the Out-islands a magistrate could require a master, on sufficient evidence, either to surrender his claim of ownership to the alleged slave, or pay the expense of sending the latter to Nassau for trial before the court specified. If the claimant secured judgment, he could bring another suit for damages, as well as for wages, for the time he had been held in bondage.[1]

Meanwhile, the planters of the Bahamas were already suffering from crop failures, and were deeply concerned over the uncertainty of the tenure of the lands which they held. After 1807 the foreign slave trade could no longer be carried on openly in the islands, and a few years later residents were claiming that their slaves had lost a quarter of the value which they possessed during the first decade of the nineteenth century. Under these circumstances, it was but natural that the slave owners, especially the refugees from the Southern states, should oppose the attempts of the English Parliament to get the colony to adopt laws for the amelioration of the condition of the blacks. These American refugees had been brought up in an atmosphere of slavery; they had been accustomed to dealing with it in their own way; and they were averse to any interference with it, especially any interference which they believed to be ruinous to their property rights, and conducive, as they alleged, to slave insurrections. The Bahama Assembly took its stand from the first against the successive measures recommended by the British government and supported by the local government. Thus a struggle began in the islands in 1815 that continued for nearly fifteen years. This struggle started with a controversy over the need of the registration of the slaves, the House of Assembly maintaining that registration was wholly inexpedient and would prove disastrous to the islands.[2]

This situation was greatly aggravated by an incident in which the attorney-general of the colony, William Wylly, a Georgia loyalist, figured so prominently that it has been designated "the Wylly affair." This incident aroused such feeling between the local legislature on the one hand and the local govern-

1. Geographical Society of Baltimore, *The Bahama Islands*, 451.
2. *Ibid*, 430, 433, 440-445.

ment on the other that legislation in regard to the registration of the slaves was precluded for a term of four years. In 1816, Attorney-General Wylly brought action to prevent a master's removal of his three negroes from New Providence to Georgia, on the ground that the slaves had been imported since the abolition of the slave trade. Two of the slaves were restored to their owner, but the third was not. The House of Assembly objected to the conduct of the Attorney-General, and also to his opinion in favor of the use of licenses and bonds for removals under the imperial statute of 1806. Its hostility was further aroused by the rumor that Mr. Wylly was in correspondence with an anti-slavery society in London, called the African Institution, which he was alleged to be keeping informed as to the colony's attitude on the question of registration.

Having determined to investigate the Attorney-General's conduct, the House undertook to summon him before a committee, only to receive an answer which it considered contemptuous. A messenger, who was sent to arrest him, was resisted by armed slaves on Mr. Wylly's premises. Outraged at this, the House next asked Governor Cameron to suspend the Attorney-General from office, and again attempted his arrest. This time it was successful, but within an hour after his imprisonment he was released by order of the Chief Justice. The House now declared the action of the Court unconstitutional, and again ordered the arrest of the released prisoner; whereupon the Governor dissolved the House. If, a few days later, the action of that body was unanimously approved by a public meeting at Nassau, the Governor had the satisfaction of receiving in due time the support of the home government. Nevertheless, the struggle was renewed by the next Assembly and its two successors.

At length, in 1818, the House passed a "healing act" under the pacifying influence of a new executive, Major-General Lewis Grant; but also voted that it could not, consistently with its dignity, and never would, grant salaries to William Wylly and the Justice of the General Court for past services since the commencement of the dispute, or for any future services. It also reasserted its claim to superiority over the courts. The uncompromising attitude of the House on these matters led to its dissolution in December, 1820. Thus, the House of Assembly spent four years in trying to override the other departments of the local government on account of the Wylly affair, and then finally adopted (1821) the system of registration for slaves.[1]

But the greater conflict was to occur over the demand for a programme of amelioration. According to this programme, which originated in Parliament and was urged by the Ministry, the flogging of female slaves was to cease; instruction was to be given to negroes in the principles of Christian morality and religion; the right to testify in courts of law was to be accorded them after they had been duly qualified to exercise such a right; the sacredness of the marriage tie was to be taught and fully protected; self-emancipation was to be encouraged, together with the accumulation of property by negroes, and too severe punishments were to be discouraged. The Bahama Assembly did not bring itself to accept these reforms until the year 1824, when it enacted a new slave code which embodied only a part of them. In 1826, however, it supplemented the code by amendatory legislation, which included almost all of the recommendations of the British government. This legislation, we are informed, "contained practically all that the Bahamas ever conceded in the enactment of regulations for the amelioration of their slaves," although "a few minor points were added in 1829."[2] But, even yet, the provision against the flogging of female slaves had found no place in the new law.

In the year last named, Sir James Smyth was sent out as governor of the Bahama Islands. His first duty was to enforce the slave code, and thus accomplish the end at which the home government had been aiming through all the previous fifteen years. As he was himself an abolititionist, he had no desire to shirk his responsibility, although he hoped to secure the coöperation of the House of Assembly in the performance of his duty. However, he soon came into a clash with that body in his efforts to prevent the flogging of enslaved women. The House brought a number of charges against the Governor, including one of mal-

1. Geographical Society of Baltimore, *The Bahama Islands*, 433-440.
2. *Ibid.*, 442, 445, 446-456.

administration, and decided to ask the King to remove him. Under such circumstances, the only thing left to Sir James was to prorogue the Assembly, which he did after a few weeks' delay. But the new Assembly, elected in 1832, was in no better mood, and the Governor found himself compelled to resort to another dissolution. In the spring of 1833, Sir James Smyth was recalled, and was succeeded by Blaney T. Balfour as lieutenant-governor. This change gave no hope of a better understanding in regard to the point in dispute between the executive and legislative departments of the colony, inasmuch as Mr. Balfour held the same convictions as his predecessor on the slavery question. Meanwhile, English sentiment had been so aroused by the failure of the colonists to enact the reforms demanded by enlightened humanitarianism that the imperial Parliament was forced to pass the statute abolishing slavery in the British Empire. Although this action was taken in the spring of 1833, the old laws governing the relation of masters and slaves were allowed to remain in force in the colonies until the first of August, 1834.[1] That the loyalist immigration was partly responsible for this result is obvious: it not only strengthened the hold of slavery on the Bahamas and the British West Indies, but also furnished a specious standard of private rights combined with public interests, under which those who had given proof of their steadfastness could do battle in behalf of a cherished but doomed institution.

V. The Loyalists in Jamaica

While we know far less of the life of the loyalists in Jamaica and the other British West Indies than of the life of those who settled in the Bahamas, the general conditions amidst which they settled are clearly distinguishable. The size of Porto Rico, together with its advantages of harbor and soil, and some doubts about the effects of Parliament's compensating the loyalists in money for their losses and sufferings led a Boston gentleman of great prominence in his day, Sir John Temple, to draw up a plan for the acquisition of this island by Great Britain, with a view to settling the friends of government there. It is not known that this project was ever submitted to the British authorities; but,

1. Geographical Society of Baltimore, *The Bahama Islands*, 480-483.

nevertheless, it is not without a certain interest for the student of loyalist affairs. Temple's project, then, contemplated the reimbursement of the impoverished loyalists partly in Porto Rican lands, instead of in money exclusively. Moreover, even those who had lost no estates were to receive grants of land. For the benefit of merchants, tradesmen, and others, a town was to be laid out and alloted to members of these classes. Such a parceling out of the island, which Temple said contained 3,290,000 acres, would enable it to accommodate 30,000 families. If negroes were to be admitted, which the author of the project thought contrary to good policy, they should be taxed; and the money secured from this source should be paid out in bounties on certain exports, such as cotton and indigo. Sugar plantations ought not to be encouraged, for England needed raw materials for her manufactures more than she needed sugar; and Porto Rico could well supply lumber and produce to the sugar islands, as well as large quantities of cotton and indigo to Great Britain. Following such a plan, Porto Rico would soon surpass Jamaica in importance. But, the land should be kept low in price, and should be subject to forfeiture if not settled within a specified period after being granted.[1]

Meanwhile, Jamaica was receiving considerable numbers of loyalists and negroes from the mainland, the great convoy from Charleston arriving on January 13, 1783. Six weeks later, the Assembly of the island passed an act for the benefit of all white refugees who had already come in, or should follow later, with the intent of becoming inhabitants. This act was made applicable to former residents of North and South Carolina and Georgia, the Bay of Honduras, the Mosquito Shore, and other parts of North America, who were paying the price of exile by being forced to relinquish their dwellings, lands, slaves, or other property. It exempted these persons for seven years after their arrival from the payment of imposts on any negroes that accompanied them, as well as from all manner of public and parochial taxes, excepting the quit rents on such lands as they might purchase or patent. It also released them from all services, duties, and offices, except the obligations to serve in the militia, and decreed that the

1. Winthrop Papers, XXIV. (In the Library of the Massachusetts Historical Society, Boston.)

charges for patenting their lands should be borne at the public expense. To avoid dispute in regard to those entitled to the benefits of the act, it was provided that all persons claiming such benefits should make affidavit, before the magistrate of the parish or precinct where they proposed to settle, of their last place of residence, the number of slaves they had brought with them, and of their intention in coming to Jamaica, this declaration to be made within three months of the passing of the act for those who had already arrived, or within the same period after their arrival for those who should come later. The local magistrates were to issue certificates to the persons satisfying the above requirements, and these certificates were to be duly recorded in the office of the secretary of the island. Loyalists who patented lands were obliged to settle and plant at least a part of these, and proceed with their improvements without intermission within two years from the date of their patents, and in default of so doing were to lose their lands. The reasons for the enactment of the above measure, which were embodied in its preamble, were that the Assembly of Jamaica felt bound by every principle of humanity to relieve and assist the suffering refugees, and that it was only good policy to give them all due encouragement, inasmuch as nothing could tend more to the security, wealth, and prosperity of the island than the increase of the inhabitants.[1]

These reasons, however, did not prevent a protest against the new law on the part of some of the older inhabitants. While applauding the law and the motives from which it sprung, the justices and vestry of Kingston presented a petition to the Assembly, November 30, 1784, calling attention to the effects of the measure upon their parish, which, they claimed, was more burdened by its provisions than all the other parishes combined. The petition explained that there were nearly seventy housekeepers in the town of Kingston who were refugees, and hence were exempt from parochial taxes, although many of these were apparently wealthy and were engaged in commerce to a considerable extent. Others were tradesmen or mechanics in the exercise of lucrative employments. Some of these persons were occupying fine houses in the best situations in the town. Thus, the petitioners were deprived of the taxes that might have accrued

1. *Acts of Assembly of Jamaica, 1778-1783*, 337, 338.

from the "opulent refugees," and were also burdened with a numerous poor of the same description, who came from the Mosquito Shore, the Bay of Honduras, and all parts of North America. The petition further recited that £1041, 11s, 4d., had been raised by subscription in Kingston for the relief of these exiles, but that the sum was so inadequate that numbers of hem still remained in the utmost distress. The parish-house was crowded with refugees, and outside support was being furnished to many others by weekly distributions of money. All this occasioned "a very great and grievous addition to the parochial taxes," in the words of the petition, from which is borrowed the annexed schedule of sums expended on the exiles in the years 1783 and 1784:

	£.	s.	d.
1783			
32 addit. pers. admitted into the parish-house, at the average of 24 l. each.....................	768	0	0
Paid for the passage of sundry refugees to other countries where they were desirous to go, & occas. necessaries; & for the temp. support of many peo. in distress.....................	127	4	2
1784			
20 addit. pers. admitted into the parish-house, to the pres. time; but in all prob. the num. will soon equal that of last year.................	480	0	0
Paid for passages and occas. necessaries..........	301	4	0
Out-pensions to refugees, about 5 l. *per* week, taking an average of two yr. for twenty-one months	455	0	0
	2,131	8	2

This petition was referred to the committee of the whole House, which was to inquire further into the state of the island but what action, if any, was taken in regard to it does not appear.[1] It is worth remarking, however, that the advent of the loyalists in Kingston had cost that parish no less than £ 3,172, 19s. 6d. in public and private contributions up to the end of November, 1784.

Other parishes in which loyalists are known to have settled were Port Royal, St. Thomas-in-the-East, St. Andrew, St. George, St. Catherine, St. Elizabeth, St. Thomas-in-the-Vale,

1. *Journals of the Assembly of Jamaica, VIII, (1784-1791)* pp. 32, 33.

and Trelawney. But, as was asserted by the justices and vestry of Kingston, the proportion of newcomers in these parishes was small in comparison with those in Kingston, probably between eight and nine per cent. of the latter number. The writer has in his possesion copies of one hundred and seventy-four of the certificates that were issued to refugees, in accordance with the act of 1783. These show that one hundred and forty-five of the recipients chose Kingston as their place of abode. Eighteen others, whose locations are given, distributed themselves over the other parishes. Sixty-one of the hundred and forty-five were accompanied by slaves, to the number of eight hundred and eighty-one. Of the eighteen others, only nine had slaves, who numbered all told five hundred and sixty-eight. While fully a fourth of these certificated loyalists had but few negroes, the rest had anywhere from five up to two hundred and over. One refugee was in charge of two hundred and two blacks, including eighty-nine of his own, who had been employed for some time on the public works, but were afterwards engaged in "jobbing" in different parts of the County of Surrey. Another refugee had brought over four hundred and twelve blacks, of whom more than half were the property of Sir James Wright, recently governor of Georgia, while another was in charge of one hundred and eighty-one, nearly two thirds of these belonging to the Hon. William Bull, late lieutenant-governor of South Carolina. Since their arrival, the last named group of one hundred and eighty-one slaves had been employed on the public works and in "jobbing" in several parishes.

A few of the exiles came from Connecticut, Massachusetts Bay, New York, and Pennsylvania, a few also from Maryland, and Virgina, but by far the greater number came from the other Southern states. Out of the hundred and seventy-four certificated loyalists, referred to above, sixty-six were from South Carolina, the most of these having come at the time of the evacuation of Charleston. Fifty-four gave the Bay of Honduras and the Mosquito Shore as their former places of residence. Among the new settlers there was a sprinkling of "gentlemen," surgeons, tradesmen, Quakers (from Philadelphia), widows, and men who had served in loyalist corps. The Quakers had been driven southward by being threatened with trials for treason. William Roach, a refugee from New York, in making affidavit before the magistrate of his parish, told of having raised a company in the corps of Loyal American Rangers, commanded by Colonel William Odell. That there were many planters among these people goes without saying. As early as January, 1784, accounts of the success of some of these loyalists in raising large crops of indigo were circulating in St. Augustine.[1] One surviving record shows that lands were granted to no less than one hundred and eighty-three refugees in the parish of St. Elizabeth. We are informed that the region in which these grants were made was little better than a morass, and that a claim for payment by the persons who surveyed and apportioned the tract led to an inquiry on the part of the House of Assembly, "when it was stated in evidence that none but amphibious creatures, such as fishes, frogs, and 'Dutchmen' could live there." It chanced that one of the loyalists who tried the experiment bore the appropriate name of Frogg, but reported in sorrow that he had buried most of his family in consequence, and that his case was only one of many.[2]

Among the refugees families that settled in Jamaica was that of Dr. William Martin Johnston, the son of Dr. Lewis Johnton, for some years treasurer and president of the King's Council of Georgia. While in the North, William became a captain in the New York Volunteers, or Third Loyal American Regiment. In 1779, Captain Johnston married Elizabeth Lichtenstein of Savannah, in whose *Recollections*, written in 1836, is preserved a record of experiences that may fairly be regarded as typical for a large class of island settlers. On the capture of Savannah by the revolutionists in July, 1782, the elder Dr. Johnston and his family were compelled to withdraw to East Florida, and until that province was ceded to Spain, he lived in St. Augustine. Captain and Mrs. Johnston, however, went fron Savannah to Charleston with the military. When, in December, Charleston was evacuated, Mrs. Johnston and her children took passage to St. Augustine to join her father-in-law's family, while her husband accompanied his regiment to New York City. Mrs. Johnston relates that she was conveyed to her destination by a small schooner, and arrived

1. Eaton, *Recollections of a Georgia Loyalist*, 218.
2. Gardner, *History of Jamaica*, 211, 212.

there safely "with many more Loyalists,' although she saw "many vessels lying stranded along the shore that had been wrecked on the sand bar." It may have been that she was writing of this dismal sight, when she remarked in a letter of January 3, 1783, to her husband: "Out of the last fleet from Charleston there have been sixteen sail of small vessels lost on and about the Bar. There are six or eight high on the beach." At any rate, she reported that no lives had been lost at the time of her own landing, although "much of the poor Loyalists' property" was destroyed.

Mrs. Johnston found St. Augustine occupied by many Greeks from Smyrna and Minorca, who had been brought there by a Dr. Turnbull to cultivate his lands on the Metanges, some miles from the city. Inasmuch as these people had failed to get along well with their employer, they had left his estates and come into town. The Johnstons remained in St. Augustine for sixteen months, during which period fish proved to be their "chief dependence and ration." With the announcement that East Florida had been ceded to the Spaniards, and that St. Augustine was soon to be evacuated, Dr. Lewis Johnston was granted a transport for his sole use "to go wherever he wished in the British Dominion." Being a native of Scotland, he chose to return to that country, and late in May, 1784, embarked at St. Mary's River for Greenock with his own and his daughter-in-law's families. Captain Johnston had sailed in advance, with the intention of pursuing medical studies in Edinburgh and London. About the same time Brigadier-General Alured Clark, formerly commandant of Savannah, was appointed governor of Jamaica. This circumstance with others, led the Captain to decide on locating in Kingston, which he accordingly did in the autumn of 1785. However, his family continued in Scotland until some time in October, 1786, and did not arrive in Jamaica until the middle of the following December. The elder Dr. Johnston spent the remainder of his life in Edinburgh, and died there, October 9, 1796.

His son was kindly received by Governor Clark, and nominally attached to a regiment in order to enable him to obtain island pay at the rate of 20s. per week for himself, 10s. for his wife, and 5s. each for his children. Not long after this he rendered important service in helping to combat yellow fever, which was brought to Jamaica from Philadephia, and according to Mrs. Johnston's *Recollections*, "made great havoc among all newcomers and sailors," although it did not attack the natives, or others who had resided there long enough to become acclimated. Later, Dr. Johnston accepted attendance on the estates of James Wildman, one of the members of the Jamaica Council, near Kingston, in St. Andrew's parish, and settled in Liguana near Halfwaytree. Here he died, December 9, 1807. In the summer of 1810, Mrs. Johnston, having arranged the affairs of her husband's estate in Jamaica, quitted the island for Nova Scotia to reside with several of her children and near her aged father, who had removed thither. [1]

The first large companies of loyalists who resorted to Jamaica were furnished provisions by the British government, but the supply soon proved inadequate. A memorial, dated April 8. 1783, was forwarded to Sir Guy Carleton at New York, signed by Charles Ogelvie, A. Wright. George Kincaid, William Telfair, John McGillivray, James Skene, J. O. Murray, Thomas Inglis, Sir James Wright, William Knox, and several others, requesting a further allowance until they could find "lands or employment, especially for their negroes."[2] Some of these loyalists secured the desired employment for their slaves, as we have already seen, by hiring them out to labor on the public works, or sending them out "jobbing," that is, to perform the heavy work on sugar and other plantations, such as digging the cane holes and planting.[3] To the extent of being able to call on the British authorities in the United States for provisions, the loyalists were fortunate; but unless their appeal was promptly answered they had to endure not only the hardships peculiar to their own lot, but also the visitations of famine and hurricane that prevailed during the early years of their residence in the islands. In part, the prospect of starvation that confronted new and old settlers alike at this time was due to the destructive effects of the hurricanes of 1780 and 1781; in part, however, it was also due to the War of Independence, to which they owed their banishment from

1. Eaton, *Recollections of a Georgia Loyalist*, 11, 12, 24, 29, 64, 73, 74, passim.
2. *Report on Am. Mss. in the Roy. Inst. of G. Brit.*, IV, 19.
3. Gardner, *History of Jamaica*, 158.

the states. Despite the proclamation of peace, the home government adopted the policy of restricting trade with the neighboring continent. An order in Council was promulgated, July 2, 1783, limiting the importation of American products (live stock, grain, lumber, etc.) into the West Indies, to British vessels, and prohibiting entirely salt beef, pork, and fish.

Whether this policy of commercial hostility towards the revolted states met with the approval of the loyalist element in the West, Indies or not, it led most of the islands to send remonstrances and petitions to the British Parliament in 1784, on the score that they were dependent on America for supplies. The Legislature of Jamaica advocated free trade with the United States as the only means of affording a chance of carrying on the island estates, of supplying their families with bread, and of averting "impending ruin." These protests were given added emphasis by a destructive storm, which occurred, July 30, 1784. This storm either sunk, drove ashore, or dismasted every vessel in Kingston harbor. It blew down public buildings in or near Kingston, and caused the loss of many lives. Indeed, the situation had become so grave by the end of the first week in August that Governor Clark exercised his discretionary power to the extent of permitting the importation of provisions in foreign bottoms during the following six months. The immediate effect of all this was to induce the planters to increase their acreage in corn and other farm produce. Scarcely had they harvested their crops when another hurricane swept over Jamaica, August 27, 1785; and the Governor found it necessary to prohibit the exportation of provisions to other suffering colonies as an alternative to opening the ports once more to American ships. Even this measure did not prevent scarcity of food during the remainder of the year, but "the climax of misery seemed to be reached" when still another storm "burst upon the land," October 20, 1786. [1] Under the drastic stimulus of these years of disaster, supplemented by the severities of the navigation laws, the islanders came to depend more on themselves, not only in raising their own provision, but also in hewing their own staves.[2] The navigation laws ceased to be enforced after 1792, and were rescinded by Parliament a few years later.

1. Gardner, *History of Jamaica*, 212, 213.
2. Edwards, *History of the West Indies, III*, 284.

It should be noted, however, that the increased production of food stuffs was not accomplished at the expense of the sugar and coffee crops, which in 1787 exceeded those of any former year. We have no means of learning how far the loyalists and their slaves contributed to these various results. Probably, they contributed their share, especially in the cultivation of coffee, inasmuch as this industry was rapidly growing in favor with the island planters at the time the exiles began to arrive. While some refugees were early reported to have raised large quantities of indigo, they must have found, as did the other cultivators, that this crop was unprofitable in the absence of protection; although it was well suited to men of moderate means and owning but few negroes. The growing of cotton, to which many of the Americans had been accustomed, proved to be only partially successful in the West Indies, on account of the variable climate of these islands.[1]

It has been truly said that in no colony did the system of slavery run more thoroughly its baneful course than in Jamaica, and in none did it die harder. As most of the loyalists who established themselves here were, or had been, slaveowners, there can be no doubt that they held the same views on the abolition of the slave-trade, the compulsory improvement of the slave code, and emancipation as did their fellow-colonials in the Bahamas. Moreover, they were now (in the year 1800) fully identified with a population of 30,000 whites, who were the proprietors of 300,000 negroes. During the previous decade, the white men of Jamaica had witnessed "the horrors which brought in the age of freedom" in the neighboring island of Haiti or St. Domingo; and they were familiar on their own soil with Maroon wars and slave rebellions. Jealous of their rights of self-government, they deeply resented England's interference with their cherished institution, which they regarded as the very foundation of their prosperity. The Assembly of the island struggled long and bitterly against the demands of the imperial government; but was compelled at last to submit to the inevitable and accept the sum of £6,000,000, or more, that was set apart as the purchase price of the slaves in Jamaica.[2]

[1]. Gardner, *History of Jamaica*, 159, 241, 242.
[2]. Lucas, *Historical Geography of the British Colonies*, *II*, 108; Gardener, *History of Jamaica*, 292.

VI. The Losses and Compensations of the Loyalists in the Islands

The losses of real and personal property sustained by many of the loyalists who fled to the West Indies and Bahamas were liberally compensated by the British government, as were the losses of those adherents of the Crown who settled in other parts of the British Empire. That the newcomers in these islands had relinquished a great amount of property is shown by the certificates issued to those who landed in Jamacia and avowed their intention of remaining as residents. As previously remarked, the writer has copies of one hundred and seventy-four of these certificates; and in one hundred and fifty-eight of them he finds evidence of the losses sustained by their possessors, definite amounts being given in one hundred and eleven certificates, while only general statements regarding the losses appear in the other forty-seven. The amounts reported range all the way from £15 up to £12,000, not a few running from £1,000 to £5,000. James Cotton of North Carolina reported the largest loss mentioned, namely, £12,000; while James Cary tells of having left Charlestown "under the necessity of abandoning all his property that he could not carry off with him, which property, so left, was confiscated by an Act of the Rebel Legislature and was of the value of £6,000 and upwards." Taking into account only the definite estimates contained in these certificates, the total amount of the losses would be £115,051, although doubtless some of the estimates were exaggerated.

A large class of claimants among the island settlers had suffered the deprivation of their property in consequence of the cession of East Florida to Spain. Four months before the definitive treaty was signed confirming this cession, the East Florida *Gazette* published a communication from Governor Tonyn in which the intended surrender of the province was announced. The communication also gave assurance that the government of Great Britain would pay every attention to the welfare of the refugees in the province, and that the Governor would exert himself in "coöperating with them to obtain a compensation for their great losses and suffering."[1]

The wretched condition of these unhappy people, for whom East Florida would soon cease to be an asylum, caused a stir in London, where the members of the Cabinet thought the matter sufficiently grave to warrant a special meeting, July 24, 1783. The purpose of this meeting was to discover some expedient for giving relief to the large number of loyalists then assembled at St. Augustine. The London papers reported that 5,000 of these people had transmitted a memorial of their distresses to the government; but that the mode of alleviation to be adopted had not yet been made known.[2]

Despite the commendable promptness of the Cabinet in considering this matter, Parliament appears to have taken no action for the financial relief of these loyalists until 1786, when it passed an act designating two commissioners to investigate the losses of such of the East Florida sufferers as might submit their claims for liquidation. For the benefit of those "proprietors" of the province who had already removed to the Bahama Islands, or other British colonies in America, the act provided that the Governor, Lieutenant-Governor, or Commander-in-Chief, and Council of such islands or colonies might act in place of the commissioners for East Florida, and that these officials should report their findings to the regular commissioners to be laid in turn before the Lords of the Treasury and the Secretaries of State. It was further provided that no claim should be received in Great Britain after January 1, 1787, or in the Bahama Islands or other colonies after March 1, of the same year. This act was to continue in force for two years after the time of its passage.[3] Early in June of the next year, however, the same measure was re-enacted for an additional twelvemonth.[4]

In the meantime, the House of Commons adopted a resolution, May, 8, 1787, recommending the granting of a sum not to exceed £13,600 to be applied in payment "for present relief and on account" to persons who gave satisfactory proof of their

1. *The London Chronicle, July 22-24, 1783.*
2. *The Morning Chronicle and London Advertiser, July 30, 1783.*
3. *Public General Acts,* 26 Geo. III, cap. lxxv.
4. *Journals of the House of Commons, XLIII,* 519.

losses to the commissioners of investigation for East Florida, this sum to be paid in proportion not exceeding 40 per centum.[1] That this amount was wholly inadequate was demonstrated by the first report of the East Florida Claim Office, which was submitted to the House at the end of May, 1788. That report showed that the number of claims received thus far was two hundred and eighty-eight, the gross amount of these claims being £602,765, 1s. 7d. of these claims one hundred and seventy nine were estimated as amounting in gross to £488,682, 1s. 7d. The losses actually allowed by the commissioners cut this last sum down to £127,552, 14s. 3d.[2] As Parliament had provided for but £13,600 of this amount at its last session, the House of Commons recommended, June 9, 1788, an additional appropriation of £113,952, 14s. 3d.[4] Later claims made necessary the voting of further sums, most of which were included in larger appropriations for groups of claimants not confined to those from East Florida. Such appropriations were made in 1789, 1792, 1793, 1794, 1795, 1796 (two), and 1798. Besides these grants "for American and East Florida sufferers" as they were designated, there was a special grant of £24,005, 12s. for East Florida claimants alone, enacted in June 1790,[5] and another of £12,262, 19s. 9d. for those from the Mosquito Shore, voted in March, 1792.[6]

One of those who received compensation was Lieutenant-Colonel Thomas Brown, who had gone to the Bahamas, and was awarded the munificent sum of $150,000 for his confiscated estates in Georgia and South Carolina.[7] Another was General Robert Cunningham of South Carolina, who was at the time a resident of Nassau, New Providence.[8] It is interesting to note that the commissioners of loyalists' claims sitting at Halifax reported at the end of September, 1786, that they had examined the cases of some few claimants of the Bahama Islands.[9] That the claims made did not always look to compensation in money is illustrated by the memorial of John Ferdinand Dalziel Smyth,[10] a Northern

1. *Journals of the House of Commons* XLII, 739.
2. *Ibid.*, XLIII, 519.
3. *Ibid.*, XLIII, 540.
4. *Annual Register* for the years named.
5. *Journal of the House of Commons*, XLV, 462, 543.
6. *Annual Register* for the year named.
7. Stark, *History and Guide of the Bahamas*, 87.
8. Sabine, *American Loyalists*, 1847, 236.
9. *Report of the Bureau of Archives, Ont.*, Pt. II, 1363.
10. In the Library of Congress.

refugee, then in England, (January 1, 1784), who in view of the important services he insisted he had rendered early and late, the great risks he had run, the captivity he had endured, the regiment of one hundred and eighty-five men he had raised for the Queen's Rangers, and the immense estate he had lost, applied to the King in Council for a grant of one of the Bahamas, named Yametta or Long Island, which contained about 20,000 acres and was still unoccupied or unpossessed, according to his representations.

The appointment of commissioners to investigate the East Florida claims aroused to action those loyalists who had lived for a longer or shorter period in West Florida. Some of "the Planters, Merchants, Public Officers, and other late Proprietors" of that province, hastening to London, presented a petition to the House of Commons, March 16, 1787, in which they set forth their reasons for asking consideration, as follows: that many loyal inhabitants of that region had joined the King's troops, and others had formed themselves into provincial corps and had been employed in dangerous service; that some of the petitioners, who had sought safety in West Florida, were now excluded from that temporary support and compensation for losses that had been granted to many refugees who had dwelt in peace and security in Great Britain during the whole War; that they had suffered serious losses, and West Florida had been surrendered under stipulations that had proved ineffectual, insofar as the loyal inhabitants were concerned; that many of these inhabitants had been reduced from affluence to indigence, while some were in want of immediate support; that no discrimination ought to be made between East and West Florida, as both had been equally loyal and and had been ceded to the enemy for the sake of peace; hence the petitioners had come to England and were asking for such relief as the House might deem proper. The House disposed of this petition, which was caustic in tone, by laying it upon the table, and nothing was heard of it afterwards.[1]

However, as we have already seen, the claims of large numbers of other loyalists were paid in money on a liberal scale. Still others

1. *Journals of the House of Commons*, XLII, 551, 552.

received compensation in the form of appointments to offices of emolument and honor under the Crown. Various executive, judicial, and fiscal positions in the Bahamas, Lesser Antilles, and Bermudas were filled in this way. Thus, in 1781, William Browne of Salem, Massachusetts, then an exile in England, was appointed governor of Bermuda. Previous to the Revolution, Mr. Browne had been a man of note in his native province, having served as colonel of the Essex regiment, judge of the Supreme Court, and a mandamus counselor. It is said that the revolutionary committee of safety offered him the governorship on condition that he support the American cause; but the loyalist declined and retired to England. His administration as governor of Bermuda began January 4, 1782, his reception by the islanders being most cordial. He conducted the business of the colony sucessfully and in harmony with the local Legislature, greatly improved the finances, and left the island in a prosperous condition when he withdrew to the mother country in 1788.[1] Another Massachusetts man who held office in Bermuda was Daniel Leonard of Taunton. A member of the General Court, he was appointed a mandamus counselor in 1774, although he never served in that capacity. In 1776 he accompanied the British army to Halifax, and doubless went thence to England. In recognition of his past services and sacrifices he was made chief justice of the Bermudas.[2]

In the Lesser Antilles, the Virgin Islands, St. Christopher's or St. Kitt's, and Antigua had loyalists among their officials. In Antigua the post of attorney to the Crown was held for some years by Samuel Quincy of Massachusetts. Like his fellow-colonials, Leonard and Browne, Quincy went to England after the evacuation of Boston, having previously been solicitor-general. He held the attorneyship of Antigua until his death in 1789.[3] Another fugitive from Boston, Nathaniel Coffin, was appointed collector of customs in St. Christopher's, a station worth £1,500 per annum, and occupied by Mr. Coffin for thirty-four years.[4] James Robertson, attorney-general of Georgia before 1779, and later a member of the House of Assembly and the Council in that province, went from New York to London in the fall of 1782,

1. Stark, *Bermuda Guide*, 1890, 51-54.
2. Sabine. *American Loyalists*, 1847, 418.
3. *Ibid.*, 551.
4. *Ibid.*, 221; Winthrop Papers, XXIV, 151.

and about a year later was appointed chief justice of the Virgin Islands with a salary of £200 per annum.¹

Besides loyalist officials, a few others of this class went to some of the islands among the Lesser Antilles. Thus, in September, 1783, the family of Captain William Sutherland of the Queen's Rangers was living in Antigua;² and, at the evacuation of New York, John Cox of New Jersey betook himself to St. John's in the same island, whence he carried on trade among the West Indies.³ In 1786, another refugee from New Jersey, James Stockton, and his sister, were residents of the Bermudas.⁴ The petitions and memorials addressed by numerous individuals at New York to the commander-in-chief, Sir Guy Carleton, during 1782 and 1783, to be permitted—if not assisted—to depart for the archipelago, the name of the particular island being omitted in most instances, suggest that Dominica, Barbados, and other islands, in addition to those named above, received a few refugee settlers.⁵

In the Bahamas at least three loyalists held offices of more or less importance. One of these was William Wylly, whose connection with the so-called Wylly affair has been previously narrated.⁶ He had been a resident of Georgia, although he spent a considerable period in New Brunswick before going to the islands. In New Brunswick, Mr. Wylly served as the first Crown counsel and registrar of the court of vice-admiralty, but in 1787 he removed to the Bahamas with his family. In the following year, he was appointed solicitor-general and surrogate of the court of vice-admiralty. In 1804, he became advocate-general of the vice-admiralty court. By 1812, he was chief justice, and two years later exchanged with the attorney-general. In 1822, he was transferred to the chief justiceship of St. Vincent, one of the islands of the Windward group.⁷ Another refugee who served as chief justice of the Bahamas was Stephen De Lancey,

1. *Second Report, Bureau of Archives, Ont., Pt. II.* 1132, 1133.
2. *Report on Am. Mss. in the Roy. Inst. of G. Brit., IV*, 374.
3. *Second Report, Bureau of Archives, Ont., Pt. II,* 929.
4. *Ibid., Pt. I,* III.
5. *Ante,* p. 15.
6. *Ante,* p. 31.
7. Lawrence, *Footprints,* 107.

formerly lieutenant-colonel of the first battalion of the New Jersey Volunteers.[1] William Hutchinson of Massachusetts also held an office in these islands.[2] Sabine thinks that Nathaniel Hall, collector of customs at Nassau, New Providence, who died in 1807, was likewise a member of a loyalist family.[3]

Jamaica furnishes at least one example of a loyalist office-holder albeit of inferior rank, in the person of Adam Dolmage, a former citizen of New York, who was appointed by the Governor on May 1, 1791, to act for twelve months as deputy registrar of the high court of chancery and clerk of the patents of this island, in place of William Ramsay, who was about to leave for England for the benefit of his health. Some years later, (that is, on January 7, 1815) Mr. Dolmage was appointed clerk of the Supreme Court, and about the same period served as clerk of the Surrey police court.[4] Isaac Hunt of Philadelphia, after being carted through the streets of that city by a mob, departed for the West Indies, where he took church orders. Subsequently, he removed to England, and became tutor in the family of the Duke of Chandos. It may be added that he was the father of Leigh Hunt, one of the most eminent literary men of England in the first half of the nineteenth century.[5]

1. Sabine, *American Loyalists*, 1847, 255.
2. *Ibid.*, 378.
3. *Ibid.*, 342.
4. Record in possession of the author.
5. Sabine, *American Loyalists*, 374.